Classic Props
InCamera Vol 3

Mike Hooks

SCOVAL
PUBLISHING LTD

British Library Cataloguing
in Publication Data
A catalogue record for this book is available
from the British Library

ISBN: 1 902236 04 1

Published by:
SCOVAL Publishing Ltd
PO Box 36
Ponteland
Newcastle-upon-Tyne
NE20 9WE
England
Tel: (01661) 820 838
Fax: (01661) 822 911

Printed in Singapore

Designed by Scott Henderson, edited by John
Wegg, and produced and typeset in 11 on 12pt
Lydian by J.P.Taylor for SCOVAL publishing Ltd

Cover Picture

BOAC's Britannia 312 G-AOVM landing at
Heathrow, probably in the late 1950s. It was
sold to Spain as EC-BSY in December, 1969.

Mike Hooks

Back Cover

Left: Welsh airline Cambrian Airways operated
ten DC-3s between November 1954 and June
1969. Landing at the airline's base at Cardiff-
Rhoose on April 16, 1965, is G-ALCC,
formerly South African Air Force 6808, which
Cambrian sold four years later to Cyprus as
5B-CAZ.

Mike Hooks

Right: Freddie Laker's Channel Air Bridge at
Southend was Silver City's rival on cross-
Channel car ferry services and had links with
SABENA. This explains the colours of Bristol
Superfreighter G-APAU (seen here at
Southend). It was replaced in 1962 by
another Bristol 170, G-APAV, until June
1966.

Mike Hooks

The InCamera Series

This is the third in an exciting range of books which sets out to portray both civil and military aircraft, both from the early days of aviation to the present day. It covers what you (the aircraft enthusiast) have said you require, no demand — the highest standards of reproduction of some of the most beautiful photographs ever taken of aircraft, in black and white or full colour, and wherever possible in large plate reproduction.

Whether you are an avid modeller, connected with aviation, or just interested in the beauty and mystique of aircraft, this new series of books in the range 'INCAMERA' will bring to you breathtaking images of aircraft reproduced to the highest standards possible today.

Classic Props InCamera

In these days of jet airliners, which to the untrained eye may all look alike, it is all too easy to forget the propeller-driven airliners which ruled supreme for so many years before the advent of jet travel. It is also easy to forget many of the airlines which flourished in the two decades after World War Two — companies like Dan-Air, Channel Airways, Eagle, BKS, Skyways, Air Charter, Silver City, Derby Airways, Air Links, Morton, etcetera in the UK, and European carriers such as Air Spain, Globe Air, Tellair, UAT, and so on. These, and others, are included within the pages of 'Classic Props InCamera', as a reminder of what air transport represented in those days.

Do you remember the big windows and wide seats of the Vickers Viscount and Convair-Liners, and the publicity shots inside Viscounts showing the almost vibration-free flight where coins could be balanced on edge and drinks showed hardly a ripple? The opening noses of the Bristol Freighters and Carvairs used on cross-Channel car ferry services where the car passengers were carried in a small cabin at the back of the aircraft? Certainly the degree of vibration in the Freighters compared very unfavourably with the turbine-powered Viscounts and Fokker Friendships.

Many photo books are commissioned, when the author takes the type of pictures perhaps required by the publisher, close-ups of detail, cockpit shots, etcetera. This book, by its very nature, is different; all of the pictures have been in existence for 30 or even 40 years, therefore most are the usual record shots taken for my own pleasure and are not 'arty' examples. I must also point out that I did not travel outside Europe in those days.

As I am an enthusiast rather than a photographer, I cannot say what exposures were needed but, with few exceptions, most were on Kodachrome film and taken with a Voigtlander Vito B or a cheap Finetta camera without the benefit of wide angle or telephoto lenses — SLRs and other advanced gadgets were beyond my means then. I have included registration details, and dates and locations wherever possible.

The result is, I hope, a book for nostalgia — it is not intended to be exhaustive but is based on aircraft which I photographed and thought were interesting. It was fun to compile and I hope that the reader gains as much pleasure in looking back on those far-off days as I have had in putting the book together.

Mike Hooks
England 1999

Left: A pair of British Overseas Airways Corporation Douglas DC-7Cs, G-AOII and G-AOIC, shot on a sunny day at the airline's London-Heathrow maintenance base, possibly in August 1958. Both were subsequently sold abroad, 'OIC to the USA as N90801 in February 1964 and 'OII to Denmark in January 1965 as OY-KNE.

Top Right: Caledonian Airways (now merged into British Airways) showed DC-7C G-ASHL at the 1963 Biggin Hill Air Fair. It was leased from SABENA from April 9 that year until it was returned to Belgium in October 1965 as OO-SFK. It went to Spain with Spantax the following February as EC-BDM.

Bottom Right: An international Douglas Commercial collection at London-Gatwick on September 20, 1964. From France, Union de Transports Aériens (UTA) DC-6B F-BGOB, Adria's DC-6B YU-AFC from Yugoslavia, Gatwick-based Lloyd International's DC-6C G-ASTW, and (in the far distance) Air Links Canadair DC-4M Argonaut G-ALHI (a DC-4 with Rolls-Royce Merlin engines). Pity that the weather was so dull!

Handley Page H.P.81 Hermes IV G-ALDT was delivered to Skyways in February 1955, one of twelve (ex-BOAC) used by this major UK charter airline, three of which were written-off in accidents. This picture was probably taken at Stansted — the company's base — on May 8, 1955. After two periods spent abroad (as OD-ACN with Middle East Airlines and VP-BBQ with Bahamas Airways) and subsequent restorations to the UK register, it was scrapped at Stansted in 1962.

Another postwar British four-engined type, the 18/20-seat Miles Marathon was similarly not a commercial success. Derby Airways (forerunner of today's British Midland) used G-AMHR 'Monsal Dale' and two others for several years before the last was withdrawn in July 1961. This photograph was taken at the airline's home base at Burnaston Airport (Derby) on August 21, 1956.

The second Vickers Vanguard built, G-APEA, is shown in BEA colours at the 1959 Paris Air Show. A Type 951, it was used for a number of demonstration flights before delivery to British European Airways. It was withdrawn from use in December 1972.

BEA's Vanguard 953 G-APES is seen landing at Heathrow and exhibiting its considerable flap area. It was later converted to freighter configuration as a Merchantman, as were several others, becoming a Type 953C. One, G-APEP, is preserved at Brooklands Museum, Weybridge, south of London.

Two Ilyushin Il-14s at Zürich, Switzerland, on June 8, 1962: MALÉV of Hungary's Il-14M HA-MAC and Il-14P SP-LNE of Polish flag carrier LOT. A Soviet contemporary of the Convair-Liner, the Il-14P could carry up to 26 passengers, while the later Il-14M, which was one metre (39 inches) longer, could accommodate 36. LOT had a mixed fleet of Soviet, East German, and Czech-built Il-14s.

Avia-14-32A OK-MZA was the manufacturer's demonstrator and is seen here at the Paris Air Show on June 14, 1959. Essentially a Czech-built Il-14M, it was a 32 seater. VIP and freight versions were among 203 Avia-14s built at Letnany.

Left: At the time of the National Gliding Championships in 1963, at Lasham, near Farnborough, Avro York G-ANTJ was one of three owned by Dan-Air which had engines and parts missing at the company's maintenance base on the airfield on May 25 of that year. Sistership G-ANTK is presently under restoration at Duxford, near Cambridge.

Top Right: The Avro Tudor graveyard at Stansted on August 18, 1956, was a depressing sight, containing long-nosed variants Mk 2 G-AGRY (in the foreground), with Mk 5s G-AKCB (ex-British South American Airways), CF-FCY (ex-Lome Airways of Canada), and one other. All were cancelled from the register in July 1959 and scrapped.

Bottom Right: The Royal Air Force Anson, in civil guise as the Avro 19, was used as an early postwar transport by several British airlines. In the absence of any colour pictures of these, here is D-IDAM at Frankfurt on July 28, 1959. Its first use after conversion from an RAF Anson (TX252) was by Railway Air Services and it later served with BEA, Airways Training, Starways, and the Swedish company Airtaco before sale to Germany in 1956.

Aer Lingus was an early customer for the Fokker Friendship. The Irish airline's attractive livery is shown on EI-AKG arriving at Cardiff-Rhoose. The airline bought seven Mk 100 Friendships — this, its last, was the 14th production aircraft. It returned to Holland as PH-FSB in January 1966.

Balair's Friendship HB-AAW is seen at Berne on April 25, 1970. It was the only airliner type serving the Swiss capital city at that time, which it did on behalf of Swissair which had no modern aircraft capable of using the short runway. Later, Dan-Air served Basle with BAe 146s.

Vickers Viking 1A G-AHOW was delivered to BEA in October 1946 and had several changes of ownership, and some trooping flights with Airwork as XD636, before sale to Trek Airways in South Africa as ZS-DKI in November 1954. It was one of very few Vikings to visit London's Croydon Airport, where it is seen here — minus port engine — on June 7, 1955. Further ownership changes followed before its withdrawal from use at Manston in February 1969.

Lufthansa Super G Constellation D-ALIN at Hannover on May 6, 1962. Withdrawn from service in mid-1967, it eventually went to a private museum in the Eifel mountains at Hermeskeil, near Trier, after display at Hamburg Airport.

An evocative line-up of Air France Constellations and Super Constellations at Paris-Orly, probably in the late 1950s. The nearest, Lockheed 749A F-BAZH, was sold to Royal Air Maroc in February 1960 as CN-CCP and was later fitted with a freight door. It was sold to Perú in August 1967 as OB-R-898. Noteworthy are the white-wall tyres of the Shell refuelling vehicles.

Top Right: Air France Super Constellation F-BGNC frames company Viscount 700 F-BGNM on the tarmac at Orly on June 21, 1955. The crew do not appear to be ready for loading and have summoned a gendarme in case of trouble!

Bottom Right: An alternative view of Constellation F-BAZH, again at Paris-Orly. The airport attracted considerable public interest as can be seen by the large crowd on the roof terrace enjoying the fresh air, unlike present day deck facilities which, if available at all, tend to be in cramped conditions behind double glazed glass screens.

The elegant lines of the Lockheed 1649A Starliner are evident in this view of N7306C of Trans World Airlines at Orly on June 17, 1959. Its last service with TWA was in April 1962 and by mid-1965 it had become the 'Flight 42' cocktail lounge in Kansas City.

The tail of TWA Starliner N7306C frames a DC-6 of French independent airline Transports Aériens Intercontinentaux (a future component of UTA) at Orly. TWA's simple but attractive colour scheme was unmistakable; an extra touch of class is apparent here — notice the curtains !

Viking 1B HB-AAR was one of two operated by Balair — the other was HB-AAN. Both were present at Basle on May 30, 1962, but returned to the UK register as G-AIVD and 'IVF, respectively, in February 1963 for Air Ferry at Manston. They were withdrawn from use there in April 1966.

Top Right: Viking 1 OE-FAE of Austrian Aero-Transport is seen at Innsbruck on June 19, 1958. Starting life as BEA's G-AHPF, it subsequently changed registration marks twice — to VP-TBC (with British West Indian Airways) and VP-YJB (with Central African Airways) — before arriving in Austria in April 1958.

Bottom Right: A former air-taxi operation, Maitland Drewery Aviation's first airliner was Viking 1B G-AHPR which was received in March 1960. When this photo was taken at Biggin Hill on May 14, 1960, it was about to re-enter service from London-Gatwick after maintenance. Compare with the shot of the same aircraft in Independent's colours on page 24.

Independent Air Transport's Viking 1B G-AHPR at Blackbushe on July 13, 1958. It survived for almost four years and three more owners before being broken up in March 1962. Following the crash of another Viking and adverse publicity, Independent became Blue-Air which ceased operating in October 1959.

Shades of Harold Bamberg's Eagle, with Viking IA G-AGRS at Blackbushe on June 7, 1958. Eagle, one of the finest British independents, operated some 140 aircraft — including 35 Vikings — in its 20 years of existence from 1948 to 1968. G-AGRS was scrapped at Southend in May 1963.

Sikorsky S-55 OO-SHE of SABENA landing at the Brussels City Heliport on June 25, 1955, on a service from Lille. The departures board showed OO-SHB to Liège, Maastricht, Cologne, and Bonn, 'SHF to Eindhoven, Duisburg, and Dortmund, 'SHA to Knokke and Vlissingen, and 'SCH to Antwerp and Rotterdam.

Top Right: SABENA's first helicopter mail service began in August 1950 with three Bell 47Ds. International flights began in 1953 when four seven-passenger Sikorsky S-55s were bought for passengers and mail services. They linked Belgium with The Netherlands, France, and Germany, and carried 18,000 passengers within the first year.

At the Brussels City Heliport we see OO-SHC, 'SHE, and 'SHF on June 25, 1955. OO-SHE is being signalled to start-up, while 'SHF (on the left) is taxiing for take-off.

Bottom Right: SABENA's Sikorsky S-55s were replaced by five 12-passenger S-58s. OO-SHL was operating a service at the Paris Heliport at Issy-les-Molineaux on May 28, 1957.

Autair International Airways (which became Court Line) ordered two HS 748 Series 2s in November 1965, receiving the first, G-ATMI, on March 30, 1966, at Luton — its home base — and the second, G-ATMJ, three weeks later. The latter was displayed at the 1966 SBAC Show in September.

Delivered to BKS Air Transport, HS 748 G-ATAM had a long and colourful history as a Hawker Siddeley demonstrator and a string of registrations, including XA-SEI, PI-C1020, 9G-ABV, OY-DFS, 9J-ABL, ZS-HSA, TR-LQY, and C-GMAA. Here it wears Merpati Nusantara titles.

To replace its Dakotas (DC-3s), Skyways Coach Air operated eight Avro (HS) 748s between April 1962 and November 1971. G-ARMW was the second to be delivered and is seen at Lympne, the company's base, in April 1966. It was sold in the Virgin Islands as VP-LVO in November 1985.

Dan-Air bought Skyways International in 1972 and, on June 5 that year, inaugurated a Gatwick — Berne service using HS 748s. G-ASPL, later named 'City of Berne', is seen at the Swiss capital's delightful airport. The aircraft was destroyed on June 27, 1981, in a fatal crash at Nailstone, Leicester, after the cargo door detached.

The prototype Handley Page Herald G-AODE, in its original form with four Alvis Leonides piston engines, was shown at the 1955 SBAC display at Farnborough in Queensland Airlines colours, somewhat optimistically as it turned out. Converted to a twin-turboprop with Rolls-Royce Darts, it was destroyed on its way to the 1958 display in a forced landing following an engine fire.

Top & Top Right: Dart-Herald G-ASBP appeared at Farnborough in September 1966 wearing the colours of Air Manila, the second of two (PI-C866 and '867) delivered to the Philippine airline that year. Both were withdrawn from use in 1972.

Bottom Right: British United Airways showed its Dart-Herald G-APWF at the Biggin Hill Air Fair in May 1964. It was broken-up at Jersey twenty years later.

Freddie Laker's Channel Air Bridge at Southend was Silver City's rival on cross-Channel car ferry services and had links with SABENA. This explains the colours of Bristol Superfreighter G-APAU (seen here at Southend). It was replaced in 1962 by another Bristol 170, G-APAV, until June 1966.

Racehorses were amongst the many cargoes carried by Bristol 170s. Here Mk 31 F-BFUO of Transports Aériens Intercontinentaux (TAI), in a rather anonymous colour scheme, loads racehorses at Le Bourget in June 1965 with a USAF Fairchild C-123 Provider in the background.

Bristol 170 Mk 31E G-AMSA of Air Charter at Southend. In the background is the once-famous Avro Tudor graveyard and a rarity, a Miles Aerovan. This 170 was converted into a Mk 32 (with longer nose) in July 1958 and was scrapped in 1967.

Channel Airways Bristol 170 Mk 21E G-AIFO at Southend served the company for nine years, from April 1957 to August 1966, after nearly the same number of years in African ownership. It was withdrawn from use at Southend in 1966.

British United Air Ferries was the result of an October 1962 merger of the cross-Channel vehicle services of Silver City and Channel Air Bridge, with BUAF being registered on January 1, 1963. Superfreighter G-ANVR 'Valiant', seen at Southend in September 1967, shows off the BUAF colour scheme. This aircraft was withdrawn from use at Coventry-Baginton in July 1972.

Superfreighters G-APAU and 'PAV subsequently entered service with Midland Air Cargo at Coventry. Both were scrapped at Lasham in May 1975 and 'PAU is shown here in August 1971, with an Avro Anson of Ekco Electronics in the background.

The ultimate development of the Bristol 170 was the Mk 32 Superfreighter which was created for Silver City Airways. It could carry three British medium-size cars and 23 passengers. Silver City operated from Lydd-Ferryfield across the Channel to Le Touquet, where G-ANWI — delivered in July 1954 — awaits loading. It became F-BKBI with Cie Air Transport in May 1961 and operated over the same route.

Top Right: Silver City Airways operated Bristol Freighters on car-ferry crossings of the Channel from 1948 until British United Air Ferries, which continued the service, took over in 1962. Six Mk 32s (all ex-British aircraft) were used by the French operator Compagnie Air Transport in similar colours to Silver City. In this photo, F-BLHH (ex G-ANWH) lands at Lydd on April 19, 1963, with the port propeller feathered.

Bottom Right: Cie Air Transport often flew its Superfreighters in tandem. Seen departing on May 26, 1962, from Le Touquet is F-BKBD, followed by F-BKBG, respectively ex G-AMWD and 'NWG.

One of three Airspeed Ambassadors used by Basle-based Globe Air, HB-IEM was present on May 30, 1962, at the Swiss company's base. All were restored to the British register by January 1964, respectively as G-ALZV, 'LZZ (HB-IEL), and 'LZS (HB-IEK).

When Globe Air decided to move into the four-engined market, the Bristol Britannia 313 was chosen and two were acquired from El Al. This shot shows HB-ITC at Basle on September 23, 1966. The company went into liquidation in 1967 following the crash of Britannia HB-ITB at Nicosia, while HB-ITC was sold in Uganda as 5X-UVH.

An interesting line-up of El Al Britannia 313 4X-AGB, and BKS Ambassador G-AMAC and Britannia 102 G-APLL. The latter was flown for two years as G-ANBG before someone realised the potentially insulting initials (No Bloody Good — at the time, because of engine troubles, the reputation of the Brit was less than stellar). The scene is London-Heathrow on March 18, 1967. The BKS Britannia was scrapped in April 1969.

Canadian Pacific Air Lines leased two Britannia 320s for eighteen months before returning them to the manufacturer for sale to Cunard Eagle Airways as G-ARKA and G-ARKB. The former is shown at Heathrow on May 26, 1963. Both were destined for Switzerland as HB-ITF and 'ITG but were not taken up, being scrapped at Coventry-Baginton in July 1971.

In August 1963, Cunard Eagle's name was changed to British Eagle International Airlines which was shortened to 'British Eagle' on its aircraft. This shot shows one of Eagle's fleet of Britannia 320s, G-ARKA at Singapore-Paya Lebar Airport on October 6, 1967.

Ghana Airways Bristol Britannia 309 9G-AAG is shown at Heathrow on May 26, 1963. Formerly G-ANCH, it was the first of two aircraft delivered to the West African airline. It was restored to the British register in June 1965 and broken up at Biggin Hill eight years later.

Left: BOAC's Britannia 312 G-AOVM landing at Heathrow, probably in the late 1950s. It was sold to Spain as EC-BSY in December 1969. The Corporation operated 33 Britannias from 1957; in its first six years, the type proved to be one of the safest airliners ever built.

Top Right: No, it is not a Britannia in spite of the colour scheme, but a Canadair CL-44D freighter leased from Seaboard World Airlines by BOAC in 1964-66.

Bottom Right: The CL-44D retained its US registration N228SW throughout its lease to BOAC. This view shows the ease with which cargo could be loaded, thanks to the swing tail.

Immaculate Britannia 312 EC-BFK of Air Spain taxis past VIASA/KLM DC-8-53 PH-DCM at Zürich-Kloten on May 19, 1968. Formerly BOAC's G-AOVE, the Britannia was sold to Spain in November 1966, initially wearing ferry registration EC-WFK.

As British European Airways withdrew its 'Elizabethan Class' Ambassadors from service with the introduction of Viscounts, the Airspeed-built airliners were snapped-up by independent airlines. BKS had five, and converted three to freighters; G-AMAC was used for passenger work from June 1960 until it was withdrawn from use at Southend in December 1968. It is seen here at Newcastle-Woolsington on July 5, 1961.

The Hampshire Aeroplane Club's de Havilland D.H.86A G-ACZP was a popular visitor to the Shackleton Sales Weekend at Oxford-Kidlington on April 24, 1958. As the last survivor of 61 built, it was all the more tragic that it rotted away at Madrid-Barajas Airport, where it was damaged beyond repair when the undercarriage collapsed on September 21, 1958.

De Havilland D.H.89 Dragon Rapide G-ALBA was the first of two used by Trans European Aviation when the company was formed at Swansea, Wales, in 1959. The Rapides were used for charter work and pleasure flying but 'LBA, seen at Biggin Hill some time between 1959 and 1961, was short-lived as it was withdrawn from use at Coventry-Baginton in September 1961.

Derby Airways acquired the former BOAC Canadair DC-4M Argonaut G-ALHS in October 1961 and used it for six and a half years. It was later scrapped at Castle Donington (now East Midlands Airport) in 1970. BOAC flew 22 of the Rolls-Royce Merlin-powered airliners.

Coventry's collection of former Trans-Canada Air Lines Canadair DC-4Ms on August 18, 1962, included CF-TFK, 'TFO, and 'TFT. They were scrapped there in 1965. British independent Overseas Aviation acquired 11 Canadian-registered examples plus nine ex-BOAC aircraft.

Left: In October 1967, BUAF simplified its name to British Air Ferries and changed its livery. Aviation Traders Carvair G-APNH, seen at Ostend, Belgium, on September 7, 1968, was damaged beyond repair at Le Touquet on March 18, 1971.

Top Right: The vehicle ferry divisions of Silver City and Channel Air Bridge were amalgamated as British United Air Ferries from January 1963. The curiously shaped ATL-98 Carvair — a DC-4 conversion dreamed up by Freddie Laker — offered greater capacity than the Bristol 170s formerly used. G-ANYB of British United is shown at Ostend on September 19, 1966.

Bottom Right: Aviation Traders Ltd converted 21 DC-4s to Carvair configuration as car ferries and freighters. British United Air Ferries operated twelve, and G-AOFW was delivered to BUAF in March 1965. It was in storage for a short time at Lydd, where it is shown in summer 1967. Although retired from service at Southend in 1978, it was not broken up until December 1983.

An early colour scheme for Finnair's Convair 440 OH-LRF, seen leaving Le Bourget on June 19 during the 1959 Paris Air Show. The airline operated a total of nine Convair-Liners; this one was sold in 1972 to Norway as LN-MTT, later serving with a number of other companies in the US and South America.

Finnair's later scheme for its Convair-Liners is shown on OH-LRB at Helsinki on September 6, 1969. This aircraft was originally built as a Model 340, the conversion to Metropolitan standard included revised exhausts, more streamlined cowlings, and extra soundproofing. Today, OH-LRB is preserved at the Finnish Aviation Museum at Vantaa Airport.

KLM's Convair 340 PH-CGB waits on a deserted ramp at Nuremberg, Germany, on April 26, 1960. Is white coat about to start the GPU? This was the second of a dozen 340s operated by Royal Dutch Airlines and it was transferred to the Dutch East Indies in May 1963 as PJ-CVB.

Saudi Arabian Airline's Convair 340 HZ-ABA was engineless at Nottingham-Tollerton on May 3, 1957, during an overhaul. It was one of nine bought new by the airline, built between batches of USAF C-131D and VC-131Ds, and this airframe was originally assigned to the USAF.

Operating a scheduled service out of Le Bourget on June 19, 1969, during the Paris Air Show, was Iberia's Convair 440 EC-AMS. One of the visible differences from the 340 was the rectangular exhausts instead of twin tubes.

JAT's colourful Convair 440 YU-ADK arriving at Zürich-Kloten on May 19, 1968, was one of eleven Convair-Liners acquired by Jugoslovenski Aerotransport, the state-owned Yugoslav airline. Total production of the Convair twin, including military variants, was 1,076.

Left: Convair 440 HB-IMM was delivered to Swissair on March 28, 1957, and named 'Valais'. Photographed at Zürich early in the 1960s, it was later converted to Rolls-Royce Dart turbine power by Aviolanda of The Netherlands. Redesignated a Convair 640, it then went to SATA, a Swiss independent airline.

Top Right: Tellair was a short-lived Swiss carrier and its Convair 340 HB-IMQ (formerly D-ACOH) was based at Basle from March 1969 until it returned to Germany in May 1970. It was photographed at Zürich on July 5, 1969.

Bottom Right: Former Swissair Convair 440 HB-IMM was re-engined with Rolls-Darts to become a Convair 640 for SATA, based at Geneva, where it was seen on April 26, 1970. On July 17, 1973, while landing at Tromsö, its undercarriage collapsed and it was damaged beyond repair.

Delivered to KLM in February 1949 as PH-TEK, this Convair 240 became PH-CEK in April 1954 with the Iranian Oil Development & Exploration Co. Allocated D-BADU for Deutsche Luftdienst, it never took up those registration marks, going instead to LOT Polish Airlines as SP-LPE on May 30, 1959. On January 17, 1968, the aircraft was sold to the US and passed through a number of US owners as N643W. It was scrapped in 1997.

Douglas C-74 Globemaster I HP-385 'Heracles' at London-Heathrow on April 6, 1963. This rare type belonged to Aeronaves de Panama which also used two others (HP-367 and HP-379) for cargo services. 'Heracles' crashed near Marseille on October 9, 1963. Only fourteen C-74s were built for the USAF.

Curtiss C-46 N9891Z flew European cargo services in Lufthansa colours in 1964 — here it is at Heathrow on August 22 of that year. The Commando was one of nine flown by Capitol Airways on behalf of the German flag carrier between 1964 and 1969.

An interesting visitor to Blackbushe, near Farnborough, on August 4, 1957, was Westair Transport Commando N4894V. It was one of many Curtiss C-46s surplus to military requirements in the early postwar years, most of the US-registered examples being freighters.

Curtiss C-46Rs of Fred Olsen Lines of Norway were occasional visitors to the UK and LN-FOP was at Southend on June 14, 1958. The Commando was a big beast, with a 108-foot (32.9m) wing span — 4ft (1.2m) more than a Boeing B-17 Flying Fortress.

Seaboard World Airlines was originally called Seaboard & Western Airlines. Here is Frankfurt-based SWA Commando N10427 at Stuttgart on April 27, 1960, which was used to feed cargo to its trans-Atlantic services. The C-46 crashed at Pereira, Colombia, on February 21, 1973, while operated by the strangely named 'Joanne Fashions'.

F-OANS was one of five de Havilland D.H.114 Heron 1Bs delivered to Union Aéromaritime de Transport (UAT) between December 1953 and March 1954. The Northrop T-38 in the background suggests that the photo was taken at the 1961 Paris Air Show.

Top Right: BEA bought two Heron 1Bs (G-ANXA and 'NXB) for its Scottish island services. They entered service in February 1955 so qualify for a mention here, although the picture shows G-ANXB on July 20, 1971, at Glasgow after they had passed to the airline's Scottish Airways Division — officially in October 1971!

Bottom Right: Morton Air Service's Heron 2 G-AOGO on a quiet corner of the Gatwick apron in September 1966. It was sold as N585PR in July 1976, one of no less than 30 which went to PRINAIR in Puerto Rico.

Douglas DC-3 G-AMVC 'Kingsford Smith' of BKS at Southend on May 25, 1957. It was involved in a trooping contract using Royal Air Force serial number XF645 in 1954 but returned to the UK civil register and was destroyed, with four fatalities, on October 17, 1961, when it crashed on Croglin Fell, Cumberland, on approach to Carlisle.

Air Links began operations in July 1959 with DC-3 G-APUC, bought from Aer Lingus. The company was Gatwick-based, but 'PUC is shown at Biggin Hill on March 24, 1962. Delivered in May 1959, it was sold in April 1964 and eventually became 5N-AAM in Nepal. A photograph of it in Aer Lingus colours appears on page 83.

Welsh airline Cambrian Airways operated ten DC-3s between November 1954 and June 1969. Landing at the airline's base at Cardiff-Rhoose on April 16, 1965, is G-ALCC, formerly South African Air Force 6808, which Cambrian sold four years later to Cyprus as 5B-CAZ.

Skyways used DC-3s on flights from Lympne to Beauvais from autumn 1955, and formed Skyways Coach-Air in 1958. This operation continued, with some breaks, until a takeover by Dan-Air in 1972. G-AMWW was delivered to Skyways in 1956 and is seen at Beauvais on June 13, 1959. After sale as EI-ARP in 1967 and restoration the same year, it later went to the USA as N2685W.

Swissair's DC-3 HB-IRX — by then in the colours of SLS, the airline's training division — outside the Pilatus factory at Stans in October 1966. Its Swiss registration was cancelled in June 1969 on sale to Ethiopia as ET-ADC, where it was destroyed by fire at Massawa on May 31, 1976, following an explosion.

When Swissair's DC-3s were withdrawn from commercial service some went to the airline's training division, SLS. This shows HB-IRN and 'IRX on the Zürich tarmac on May 19, 1968. The former aircraft is preserved in the Verkehrshaus der Schweiz at Luzern — do not be misled by DC-3 N65371 displayed at Munich Airport as 'HB-IRN'!

April 25, 1964, a dull day at Amsterdam-Schiphol with Martin's Air Charter DC-3 PH-MAA and Canadian Pacific Air Line's DC-8-43 CF-CPI, the Canadians apparently preferring Esso to Martin's choice of Air BP! Cancelled from the Dutch register in October 1967, the DC-3 became HB-ITD for several years before export as N37737. It was last reported derelict at Mexico City in January 1979.

Top Right: Air France DC-3 F-BAXP was one of three engaged in training flights at Cormeilles-en-Vexin (more familiar these days as Pontoise) on May 27, 1957. The all-silver scheme contrasts with the white cabin top adopted later.

Bottom Right: DC-3 F-BEIG shows signs of its Air France ancestry at Le Bourget in June 1967. It was finally retired from service by Stellair of Norway on October 9, 1989, and acquired by the SABENA Oldtimers Association.

Hunting Aerosurveys and Geophysics used DC-3 G-AMYW for aerial survey work, hence the strange structure on the fuselage. It is seen at Croydon on February 11, 1956, with several Transair DC-3s in the background. It crashed in Saudi Arabia on April 8, 1967, still in the service of Hunting.

Aer Lingus DC-3 EI-ACH gleams as it approaches to land at Heathrow on August 21, 1956. It became G-APUC in June 1959 and was sold to Royal Nepal Airlines in April 1964 as 5N-AAM. Aer Lingus originally registered it on January 30, 1946, a conversion from a USAF C-47A, 42-93038.

Kar-Air's DC-3 OH-VKB glistens on the tarmac at Helsinki on September 7, 1969. Formerly SE-BAC, it was registered in Finland on April 26, 1957, to Kar-Air. Withdrawn from service in November 1979, it was donated to the Finnish Aviation Museum at Helsinki-Vantaa where it is presently displayed.

Iberia's Douglas DC-4 EC-AEO on final approach — probably at Gatwick on July 22, 1961 — went to Aviation Traders in November 1964 for conversion to a Carvair. It became EC-AZA and made its first flight in this form on March 12, 1965. Note Iberia's fleet number on the fin.

Aer Turas DC-4 EI-AOR passed through various hands before reaching the Irish independent airline in June 1965. Here it is at Cardiff-Rhoose with a locally based Cambrian DC-3. Formerly F-BIUT, this DC-4 was sold to South Africa in December 1969 as ZS-IGC.

The placard writers have got it wrong — this much-labelled DC-4 is TMA's OD-ADK on lease to Craven Filters King Size at the Biggin Hill Air Fair in May 1965. Trans Mediterranean Airways began operations out of Beirut with Avro Yorks in 1953, later buying two DC-4s, one of which was destroyed in the Israeli attack on Beirut Airport in December 1968, along with a TMA DC-6.

G-APCW was one of two DC-4s operated by UK independent Continental Air Transport. It is shown at the end of Southend's runway on September 18, 1960, a mere twenty days before the company ceased operations. It later became 90-PCW of the Congolese Air Force.

Top: UK charter airline Lloyd International Airways was founded in January 1961 and initially operated three Douglas C-54 Skymasters including G-APID, leased for several months from Trans World Leasing. Here it lands at Heathrow on May 21, 1962; it was sold to Spain in August 1967.

Top Right: Independent Air Travel DC-4 G-APNH at Blackbushe on February 28, 1959. Later passing to Air Charter then British United Air Ferries, it was subsequently converted to a Carvair.

Bottom Right: Following nine years of service with KLM, first as PH-TFH and then PH-DFH, this DC-6B was sold to Yugoslav charter company Adria Aviopromet as YU-AFC in August 1961. It is seen at a dull Gatwick on September 20, 1964, with the nose of Lloyd International's DC-6C G-ASTW in the background.

Air France DC-4 F-BBDQ at Orly on June 21, 1955. In the background is Pan American Boeing Stratocruiser N1037V and Lufthansa Convair 340 D-ACEF. DC-4s formed the backbone of Air France's long-haul fleet early in the 1950s until replaced by Constellations.

Pan American Douglas DC-6B N5120V 'Clipper Mermaid' is seen landing at Heathrow on April 16, 1955 — almost a year after its delivery.
It subsequently served with a number of companies and in several countries before sale to Perú.

Originally CF-CUS with Canadian Pacific, DC-6A F-BGSK passed through a number of other owners before reaching Aéromaritime/UAT in whose colours it is seen at Le Bourget on June 1, 1957, during that year's Paris Air Show.

The colourful scheme of Ethiopian Airlines worn by DC-6B ET-T-26 on July 27, 1959, when the aircraft was just over a year old. It was burnt-out in a landing accident at Asmara in March 1970. EAL had three DC-6Bs; its other two were replaced by Boeing 720Bs in 1962.

SABENA's DC-6B OO-CTN at Zürich on June 6, 1962. It served for some months in 1964 with Caledonian Airways as G-ASRZ before returning to Belgium. Sistership OO-CTK was also with Caledonian in 1964 as G-ASTS. The light aviation hangar in the background also housed the airport's fire service but is now long gone.

DC-6B SE-BDS 'Vidar Viking' of SAS landing at London-Heathrow. It finished its career in April 1963 when operated by Syrian Arab Airlines as YK-AEB, catching fire on take-off at Hama, Syria.

Left: Delivered new to Swiss Air Lines (as the company then styled itself), DC-6B HB-IBO prepares for loading on the ramp at Zürich on July 25, 1954. It served with Finlantic of Finland for 14 months before returning to Switzerland, eventually going to Greece as SX-DAM.

Top Right: Swissair DC-6B HB-IBI shares the tarmac at Zürich with a company Convair 440 Metropolitan and Aer Lingus Viscount 800 EI-AKO on June 8, 1962. The DC-6B crashed during a three-engined landing at Copenhagen in April 1963.

Bottom Right: Balair's DC-6B HB-IBU seen against a stormy sky at Basle on April 26, 1970. Delivered new to Swissair in November 1953, it was passed to the flag carrier's charter subsidiary in 1962 and was broken up ten years later.

An unusual visitor to Paris-Le Bourget on June 14, 1959, was Guest Aerovías DC-6 XA-MUK. It was not quite as exotic a visitor to Europe as it seemed, perhaps, because it had been sold to México a few weeks earlier by SAS with which it served as SE-BDC then OY-KLY.

DC-6Bs TF-OAA and 'OAB are seen in UNICEF colours at Basle on April 26, 1970. They were both originally with Western Air Lines then Japan Air Lines where their paths diverged. They were reunited in May 1969 in Iceland under Fragtflug ownership as TF-FRA and 'FRB respectively, and began UNICEF operations in February 1970.

Norwegian DC-4 LN-HAT of Braathens SAFE was hired to Icelandic Airlines-Loftleidir in whose colours it is seen at Luxembourg on August 8, 1959. It was sold in April 1961 to the French Navy. Number three engine seems to be a problem here.

Loftleiðir's DC-6B TF-LLE at Luxembourg on June 19, 1962. Serving with Pan American from May 1954, it was sold to Loftleiðir in March 1962 and subsequently served with Transavia Holland as PH-TRL and Aid by Air as TF-AAB.

UTA's DC-6B F-BGSN was leased in 1961 to Libiavia, an independent airline from the Kingdom of Libya, and subsequently passed to Air Afrique and Olympic Airways. It was on the Le Bourget tarmac during the Paris Air Show in early June 1961. On the left is Dove G-AJGT of the De Havilland Engine Company.

This postwar-built DC-4 was the last of four originally delivered to Trans-Australia Airways as VH-TAA to 'TAD. It was a visitor to the 1961 Paris Air Show in its US markings with Trans Atlantic Airlines — the same initials as its former Australian owner, but on the other side of the world. In the background is an Aéromaritime DC-6 and the experimental Nord 1500 Griffon.

Aer Lingus was the third customer for the Vickers Viscount — after BEA and Air France. Type 808 EI-AKL shares the Heathrow tarmac with three BEA Viscounts on April 26, 1959. It was sold to West Germany in March 1970 as D-ADAM.

This shot of Cunard Eagle's Viscount 755 G-AOCB was taken at Heathrow on May 26, 1963. At this time it was on its third registration, having previously been CU-T604 of Cubana and VR-BBL of Eagle Airways (Bermuda). In April 1970, after 14 years of operation, it was withdrawn from use at Castle Donington (now East Midlands Airport).

Lufthansa Viscount 814 D-ANIZ was at Schiphol with a pair of KLM Viscount 800s on April 25, 1964, and a motley collection of DC-3s in the background. This northern apron of Amsterdam's airport is now used for general aviation.

After BEA, KLM was the second customer for the Viscount 800 series. One of its 803s, PH-VIG, was photographed at Zürich on September 28, 1966. It subsequently went to Aer Lingus as EI-AOM, but crashed following a mid-air break-up over the Irish Sea on March 24, 1968, with 61 fatalities.

BEA's Viscount 701 G-ANHF is seen with some of the airline's DC-3 fleet at Heathrow. The airport was still under construction — in fact it is still not finished! The Viscount was sold to VASP, Brazil, in July 1963 as PP-SRR.

Top Right: BEA Viscount 802 G-AOHO 'Samuel Wallis' is seen landing at Heathrow. It was withdrawn from use at Cardiff-Rhoose in March 1976.

Bottom Right: British European Airways operated more than 70 Viscounts early in the 1960s, both Type 700s and 800s. The Corporation's 'red square' colour scheme is seen on Viscount 806 G-AOYT at Gatwick in April 1966 with the company's ground handling equipment and awaiting passengers. It was sold to Taiwan as B-3001 in May 1969.

Turk Hava Yollari-Turkish Airlines received five Viscount 700s in 1958 for its European routes and TC-SEL, seen at Istanbul-Yesilkoy in October 1970, was the third. Two were lost in crashes, but TC-SEL, 'SEC and 'SES were sold to the Turkish Air Force in 1971; two remained in service into the 1990s.

Iraqi Airways bought three Viscount 735s and the second of these, YI-ACL 'Sinbad', rests outside BOAC's Heathrow base on September 4, 1956. A fourth Viscount, Type 773 YI-ACU, was acquired later. The airline's first Viscount service was to London via Istanbul and Vienna.

Air France operated twelve of the double-deck Breguet 763 transports from 1953 — initially with 59 passengers on the upper and 48 on the lower deck. Six were eventually sold to the French Air Force while the other six were converted to cargo configuration with the type name 'Universal'. F-BASV was one of the latter batch and is seen here at Le Bourget. It was scrapped at Toulouse in 1969.

SNCASE SE 2010 Armagnac F-BAVH on a dull day at the Paris Air Show on June 19, 1955. SAGETA was founded by Air France, Aigle Azur, TAI, and UAT and used seven Armagnacs (only nine of the type were built) during the war in Indo-China, operating between Toulouse and Saigon. F-BAVH was scrapped in 1961.

The International Red Cross used four Swiss-registered Boeing C-97G Stratofreighters from April 1969 for relief work. HB-ILZ is seen at Basle being operated by Balair. Formerly USAF 52-0857, it was, like the other aircraft, returned to the USAF on June 24, 1970.

The Boeing Stratoliner was a distinct rarity. F-BELY of Airnautic was based at Le Bourget in 1961 at which time four were still flying in Europe; they were originally operated by Aigle Azur. The photograph was taken at Le Bourget on June 9, 1963.

Allison engines whining, KLM's first Lockheed 188C Electra, PH-LLA 'Mercurius', leaves Le Bourget on June 13 during the 1963 Paris Air Show. It was sold to Universal Airlines in the US in March 1968 as N851U and converted to a freighter. In 1972, it was written off in an accident and part of the fuselage was used to rebuild another Electra.

Top Right: SABENA was the third European operator of the Convair 240 and, after six new aircraft had been delivered, bought N1820 from Texaco in March 1955, registering it as OO-AWV. Seen at Brussels on June 24, 1955, it was sold to Ethiopian Airlines as ET-T-22 in July 1956. Following a number of ownership changes, it was destroyed by fire in a forced landing at Clewiston, Florida, on September 4, 1978.

Bottom Right: Following the end of production of Convair 440s, General Dynamic's subsidiary Canadair acquired three unsold aircraft for re-engining with Napier Eland turboprops as the CL-66C, marketed as the Convair 540. Canadair also sold ten conversions to the RCAF as CL-66Bs (CC-109s). Napier's 540 demonstrator (G-ANVP), formerly a 340, joined an Airspeed Ambassador and Vickers Varsity in 1956 as a testbed for the Eland. The aircraft was transferred to the US as N340EL in October 1957 and was demonstrated at the 1959 Paris Air Show, as seen here. Following the takeover of Napier by Rolls-Royce, the engine programme was abandoned and all non-Canadair converted aircraft reverted to 440 standard.

Overwhelming everything at the 1969 Paris Air Show was the Antonov An-22 SSSR-56391. The RAF HS 125 Dominie lends scale to the picture. The prototype An-22 had first been shown at Paris in 1965, less than four months after its first flight, taking the press by surprise — quite an achievement.

Antonov An-12 SSSR-11031 outside BEA's maintenance base at Heathrow in November 1967. Close examination reveals the constructor's number on the fin as 7345003 and the Aeroflot title in small letters plus winged logo are beneath the cockpit. This version has a neat fairing in place of the tail turret. Three years later, this aircraft was destroyed in a take-off accident.

Aeroflot Ilyushin Il-18D SSSR-75581 was shown at the 1965 Paris Air Show. This was the long-range version of the 'Soviet Electra' with maximum seating of 122. Il-18s captured a number of closed circuit speed records with payloads in 1959-60. The nose of a Royal Air Force 111 Squadron English Electric Lightning is prominent on the right.